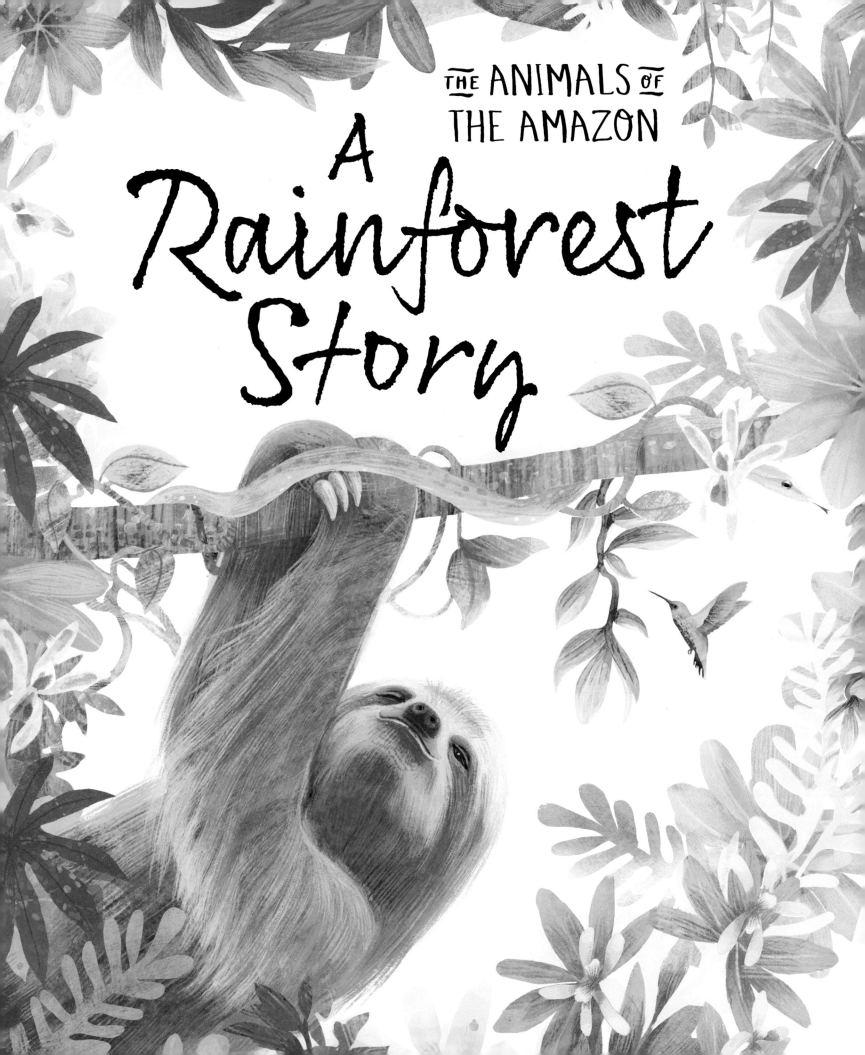

THE ANIMALS OF THE AMAZON

A Rainforest Story

For all the animals of the rainforest and
every person who works to protect them —J.B.
For C.B. —K.B.

A Raspberry Book
Art director and cover designer: Sidonie Beresford-Browne
Designer: Nicky Scott
Author: Jane Burnard
Editor: Tracey Turner
Illustrator: Kendra Binney
Consultant: Paul Lawston

Text and design copyright © Raspberry Books Ltd. 2024
First published 2024 in the United States by Kingfisher,
120 Broadway, New York, NY 10271
Kingfisher is an imprint of
Macmillan Children's Books, London

Distributed in the U.S. and Canada by Macmillan,
120 Broadway, New York, NY 10271

EU representative: 1st Floor, The Liffey Trust Centre,
117-126 Sheriff Street Upper, Dublin 1 D01 YC43

Library of Congress Cataloging-in-Publication Data has been applied for.

ISBN 978-0-7534-8005-2

Kingfisher books are available for special promotions and premiums.
For details contact: Special Markets Department, Macmillan, 120 Broadway,
New York, NY 10271

For more information, please visit
www.kingfisherbooks.com

Printed in China
1 3 5 7 9 8 6 4 2
1TR/0124/RV/WKT/140MA

MIX
Paper | Supporting
responsible forestry
FSC
www.fsc.org   FSC® C116313

THE ANIMALS OF THE AMAZON

A Rainforest Story

WRITTEN BY
JANE BURNARD

ILLUSTRATED BY
KENDRA BINNEY

KINGFISHER
LONDON & NEW YORK

HARPY EAGLE

SCARLET MACAWS

SQUIRREL MONKEYS

CAPUCHINS

KINKAJOU

GIANT ANTEATER

LEAF-CUTTER ANTS

YAPOK

POISON DART FROG

GREEN VINE SNAKE

SLOTH

TOUCAN

This is the AMAZON RAINFOREST.

A rich, wet, tropical jungle, full of plants and snaking waterways.

It's gigantic, sweltering hot, and full of animals.

They are made for this place, and it is made for them.

JAGUAR

BLUE MORPHO BUTTERFLY

HUMMINGBIRD

PIRAPUTANGA FISH

BLACK CAIMAN

MANATEE

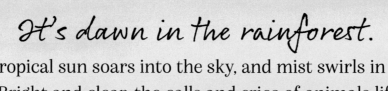

It's dawn in the rainforest.

The hot, tropical sun soars into the sky, and mist swirls in wisps over treetops. Bright and clear, the calls and cries of animals lift from the forest, filling the air with howls, hoots, shrieks, and whistles.

The rainforest **CANOPY** is a great green ocean, spreading in every direction as far as the eye can see. Now and then giant trees rise above it, like watchers guarding the forest.

Suddenly, a pair of **SCARLET MACAWS** burst up from the treetops. They flap toward a hole in one of the tallest trees, crimson tail feathers streaming.

Quick as a wink, they disappear inside.

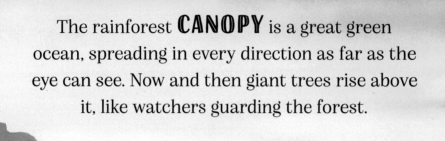

But they've been spotted by a pair of fierce, sharp eyes.
A **HARPY EAGLE**, deadly predator and ruler of the
Amazon skies, pushes off from her own towering perch.
She preys on many animals, including parrots.

Scarlet macaws are parrots that can live for more than forty years.
They are sociable, intelligent birds, forming lifelong partnerships with
their mates. They like to keep the same nesting places year after year,
often choosing hollow trees. Their strong beaks are made for
cracking open hard-shelled nuts and seeds.

Inside the hollow, two chicks, with their eager beaks and bright, excited eyes, squeak and clamor for food. They can fly short distances now, but they're not quite ready to fend for themselves. Their parents chirr reassuringly and feed them the fruit and seeds they gathered earlier.

SQUIRREL MONKEYS

The eagle soars around their tree. But leaves are shaking in the treetops beneath. **SQUIRREL MONKEYS** are leaping lightly from branch to branch, stuffing handfuls of fruit into their mouths. Angry **CAPUCHIN MONKEYS** rush, squealing, to see them off. This is their patch. Still gobbling fruit, the squirrel monkeys scamper onto higher, thinner branches.

Squirrel monkeys are one of at least 130 different types of monkeys in the Amazon. Like many other rainforest animals, they spend almost all their lives in the treetops, or canopy.

CAPUCHIN MONKEYS

Seizing her chance, the eagle dives and smashes through the canopy, huge claws stretched out to grab a squabbling monkey . . .

Harpy eagles can measure over 3 feet (1 m) tall and are adapted for flying through the tangle of plants in the rainforest. They snatch animals—especially monkeys—in their huge talons.

But the monkeys are faster.

In a flash, the tree empties and the harpy eagle comes crashing out of the canopy. A screaming capuchin baby is left hanging by his tail, grasping for handholds. His mother stretches out and snatches him to safety.

The capuchins settle in lower, safer branches to groom, snooze, and play. The mother holds her baby and gazes lovingly into his eyes, gently smacking her lips. But he wiggles away. Like all capuchins, he's smart and inquisitive, and he wants to explore.

He finds a **TANK BROMELIAD**, a plant with a hollow center full of rainwater. He sees something moving on a leaf and bends closer. A tiny, fearless frog stares back. Shrieking in alarm, the capuchin's mother yanks her baby away—those colors spell danger.

Capuchin monkeys are highly intelligent. They've been seen using simple tools, such as stones, to crack open nuts, and rubbing special leaves on their faces to ward off skin infections and mosquitoes. Their strong tails grip branches like hands, giving them extra treetop support.

TANK BROMELIAD

It's midday, hot and still.

Rain patters above and drips from the ends of shiny green
leaves, and the canopy air is wet with water vapor.
Thick, twining vines called **LIANAS** snake through the
treetops. Branches and trunks bristle with plants that live
without soil—orchids, ferns, and bromeliads.

The small, brightly patterned animal is a
POISON DART FROG, with a single tadpole riding
on his back. He climbs down inside the bromeliad and
the tadpole wiggles free, hitting the water with a plink.
It joins tiny shrimp and larvae, and a rotting leaf—

plenty for it to eat in here.

Now the male frog walks the long 30 feet (9 m) down the trunk to the ground to collect another tadpole and drop it into another treetop bromeliad. On the way, a deadly **GREEN VINE SNAKE** swerves to avoid him.

No one messes with a poison dart frog.

ORCHIDS

FERNS

Amphibians like frogs thrive out of water in humid rainforests. Poison dart frogs' bright colors are a warning that they are highly poisonous. Female frogs lay up to six eggs. When the tadpoles hatch, their father carries them one by one up to treetop tank bromeliads, where they develop into frogs.

The vine snake loops and slithers along a branch, like a green ribbon through leaves. Her forked tongue flickers up and down to taste the air.

A dozing three-fingered **SLOTH** is hanging in a patch of afternoon sunlight as the snake skims right over his curling claws. A sleepy eye opens in the sloth's smiling, oval face, and the snake goes gliding on.

The green vine snake hides among canopy leaves and flowers, waiting for small animals to come close. Then it strikes—fast. Two large fangs inject its prey with poison.

She freezes at the end of the branch,
looking just like a stalk among the leaves.
A hovering **HUMMINGBIRD**, swift
and bright, is about to visit a flower.
Unlike the sloth, this little creature is always
moving and needs plenty of sweet nectar
to fuel her whirring wings.

The snake holds very still
but, sensing something, the hummingbird
darts backward and away.

This hummingbird is a
blue-chinned sapphire. All
hummingbirds have long beaks
and tongues to probe inside
flowers. Their wings beat up to
80 times per second, with a
figure-of-eight motion that gives
them perfect control in the air.

The sloth uses his long arms and hooked claws to haul himself steadily around the canopy, sampling leaves. Moths flutter from his shaggy coat, which is tinged green with algae.

A dull-brown **BUTTERFLY**, with dark, eye-like wing spots, rests on a twig in front of the sloth. Suddenly, in a brilliant blaze of blue, it spreads its wings and takes off. The sloth turns his head to watch as it goes flashing away.

Sloths move very slowly around the canopy, putting a lot of their energy into digesting leaves. Their fur is home to moths and beetles, as well as green algae, which provides camouflage.

Far below them, glimpsed through layers of leaves, is the dim, damp forest floor. Raindrops drift down from the canopy above, and mushrooms sprout in leaf litter. But a hurrying trail of emerald-green leaf shapes, like a flotilla of little sailboats, lights up this gloomy place.

Blue morphos are one of the largest butterflies in the world. As they fly, the bright blue inside their wings flashes on and off, so they seem to appear and disappear.

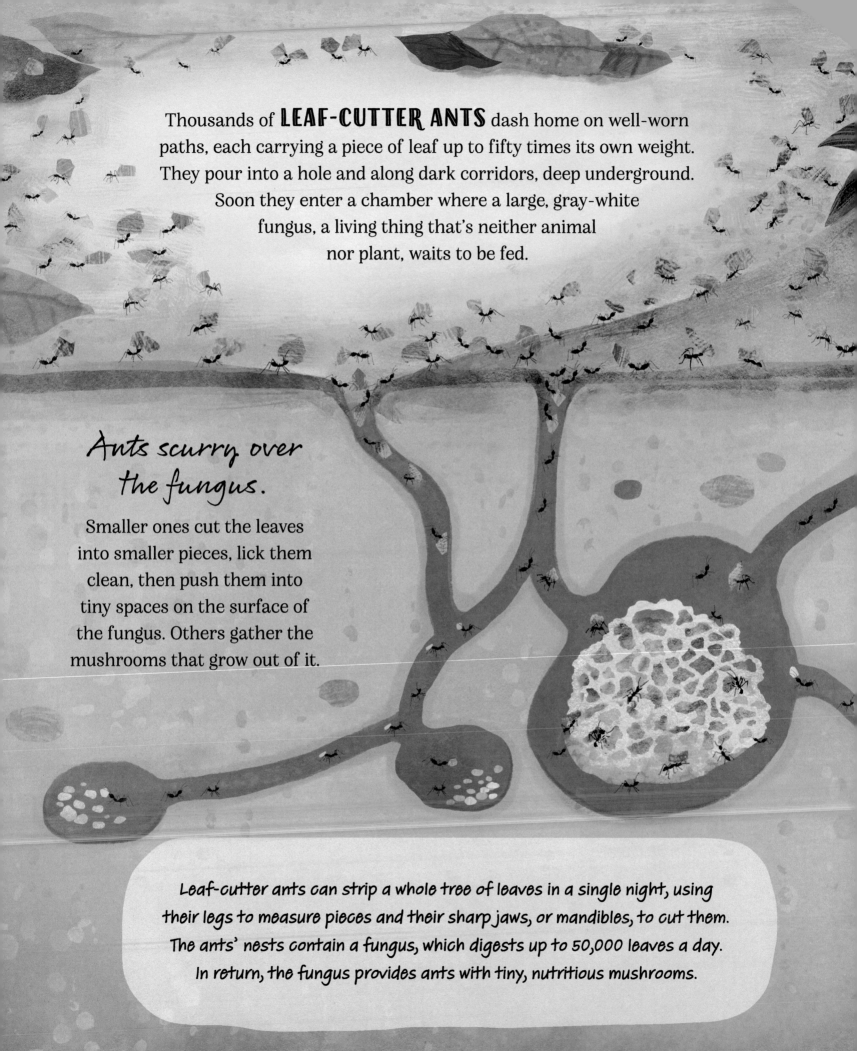

Thousands of **LEAF-CUTTER ANTS** dash home on well-worn paths, each carrying a piece of leaf up to fifty times its own weight. They pour into a hole and along dark corridors, deep underground. Soon they enter a chamber where a large, gray-white fungus, a living thing that's neither animal nor plant, waits to be fed.

Ants scurry over the fungus.

Smaller ones cut the leaves into smaller pieces, lick them clean, then push them into tiny spaces on the surface of the fungus. Others gather the mushrooms that grow out of it.

Leaf-cutter ants can strip a whole tree of leaves in a single night, using their legs to measure pieces and their sharp jaws, or mandibles, to cut them. The ants' nests contain a fungus, which digests up to 50,000 leaves a day. In return, the fungus provides ants with tiny, nutritious mushrooms.

Bigger ants with vicious jaws surge upward to defend their nest. Huge claws, powered by strong arms, are breaking it open from above, and a long, sticky tongue is flicking down tunnels, dragging out ants.

It's a giant anteater, carrying her pup on her back.

The snuffling anteater sucks up hundreds of ants before the biting defenders drive her off. Then she lumbers down to the river to drink.

As they leave the shelter of the trees, the baby raises its head and blinks in sudden, *late-afternoon sunlight.*

Anteaters use their powerful claws to dig into ant and termite nests, then flick their long tongues to pull ants from their tunnels. They only take a few hundred ants at a time, though the nest contains millions, allowing the ants to rebuild their home and replace lost ants.

Water runs crystal clear before them, and waterweed ripples bright green. A **TOUCAN** reaches out to pull a ripe berry off a fruit tree, knocking several into the water as he does so.

Beneath him, excitement stirs. **PIRAPUTANGA** fish swirl in the water, their silvery backs breaking the surface as they gobble up the dropped fruit. Suddenly, one of them shoots up from the water, golden tail whipping. It snatches a sprig of berries from the tree, and the toucan flaps away, squawking.

Piraputanga love eating fruit, and some have learned how to leap up and grab it from trees.

The piraputanga cruise upstream now, heading for the shallow place where they lay their eggs. They pass a peaceful pool where giant water lilies rest on the surface and purple hyacinths bloom.

Large, gray bodies, lit by the setting sun, move slowly beneath the water. It's a pair of **MANATEES**, gentle creatures with tiny eyes, using flippers and tails to scoot gracefully around the pool's bed, grazing on underwater greens.

Nearby, a **BLACK CAIMAN** slips into the water. He's after the piraputanga— the manatees are too big for him.

Black caiman are a type of alligator that can grow up to 20 feet (6 m) long. They hunt fish and land animals that come too close to the water.

A **JAGUAR** reclines on a sturdy branch. Her limbs ripple with muscles, and she wears a beautiful patterned coat that mimics dappled shade. She's the queen of the jungle, and this is her throne. Although she often hunts in water, the manatees are too big for her, too.

Manatees are related to elephants. Like elephants' trunks, their wide, whiskery muzzles are very sensitive and can be used like a hand to greet each other or to pull up waterweed.

The sun has set, and darkness cloaks the riverside. Different animals come alive at night, and the jungle bursts with new sounds. Male frogs, each trying to be the loudest, croak, buzz, and squeak to attract mates. Cicadas sing. And a spectacled owl cries,

"Hoo-hoo-hoo-hoo-hoo."

Beneath the moon and stars, fireflies flash on and off in trees, and glowworms and railroad worms gleam. Even mushrooms glimmer green.

The jaguar is creeping forward, entering shallow water on stealthy, silent paws.

She pounces . . . on the caiman.

The two mighty animals twist and crash, splashing and struggling against each other. But the jaguar grips the caiman's head in her powerful jaws and bites down until he's still. Then she drags him away to eat.

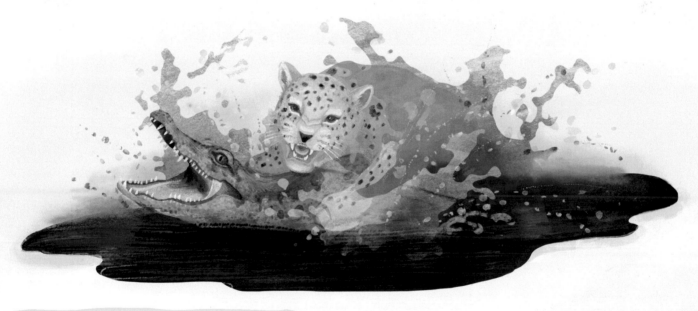

Jaguars are strong, ferocious hunters, with the most powerful bite of any big cat—often taking on prey three or four times their own weight. They live alone and mark the edges of their territory with their waste, or by scratching trees.

Some time later,

a little **YAPOK** feels its way to the water's edge.

The yapok keeps her eyes tight shut underwater. Long tail
swishing, she swims with arms outstretched, her sensitive fingers
and whiskers feeling for underwater prey. She swerves suddenly,
grabbing a small fish in her pointy jaws.

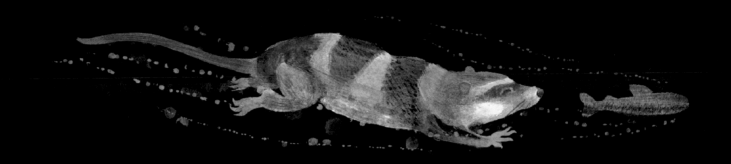

Back on shore, four baby
yapoks climb out of a pouch
on her front and clamber
onto her back while she
munches her meal.

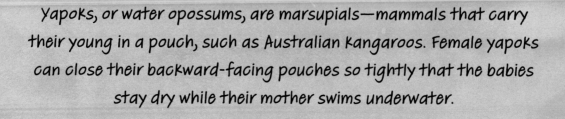

Yapoks, or water opossums, are marsupials—mammals that carry
their young in a pouch, such as Australian kangaroos. Female yapoks
can close their backward-facing pouches so tightly that the babies
stay dry while their mother swims underwater.

Up in the treetops,
furry **KINKAJOUS** come slinking along branches.
A balsa tree has come into bloom—a very special event.
The kinkajous are here to sip the rich, sugary nectar
that flows from its large, cup-like flowers.

The night sky is thick with **MOTHS**
and teeming with the bats that hunt
them. But some bats, like Pallas's long-
tongued bat, eat nectar, too. They hover
around the tree and sip with the kinkajous.

It's a sweet feast that
lasts all night long.

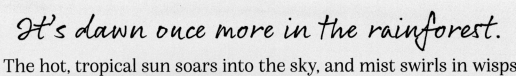

It's dawn once more in the rainforest.

The hot, tropical sun soars into the sky, and mist swirls in wisps over the treetops. Kinkajous curl up fast asleep in their nests.

Today the young macaws are ready for an important journey. Their watchful parents lead the way as other parrots join them in the air, heading for the same place . . .

Kinkajous are related to raccoons. They enjoy eating sweet fruit, nectar, and honey.

. . . a high riverbank,
ablaze with jewel-colored birds.
Parrots break off and gulp down the
clay they need to survive.

The youngsters swoop down after their
parents to join the squawking crowds.
In time, these brilliant birds will find their
own partners and raise their own young.
Then they'll bring them here, too.

And all around, bright and clear, the
calls and cries of animals lift from
the forest, filling the air with
*howls, hoots, shrieks,
and whistles.*

Generations of Amazon rainforest parrots regularly visit the same places—
called clay licks—to eat clay for the minerals it contains, which they need to
help them grow and thrive. Some fly over 50 miles (80 km) to get there.

This is the
AMAZON RAINFOREST.

A rich, wet, tropical jungle, full of
plants and snaking waterways.

It's gigantic, sweltering hot,
and full of animals.

They are made for this place,
and it is made for them.